FISH FOR KIDS

Swim like a bluespotted stingray, page 9

FISH FOR KIDS

A JUNIOR SCIENTIST'S GUIDE
to Diverse Habitats, Colorful Species, and Life Underwater

JUNIOR SCIENTISTS

KEVIN KURTZ, MA

ROCKRIDGE PRESS

To all my fishy friends in the South Carolina Marine Educators Association (SCMEA).

Series Designer: Junior Scientist Design Team
Interior and Cover Designer: Linda Snorina
Art Producer: Meg Baggott
Editors: Grace Jeong and Nicky Montalvo
Production Editor: Jenna Dutton
Production Manager: Riley Hoffman

Illustrations Kate Francis ©2021, Photography imageBROKER / Alamy, Cover, p. vi; Martin Strmiska / Alamy, p. ii; Shutterstock, p. viii, 10, 14, 17, 21, 29, 34, 36, 37, 38, 40, 41, 43, 45, 47, 48, 49, 50, 51, 52, 53, 56, 58, 61, 62, 63, 64, 65, 68, back cover; Stocktrek Images, Inc. / Alamy, p. 4; The Photolibrary Wales / Alamy, p. 6; Jaap Bleijenberg / Alamy, p. 10; VPC Animals Photo / Alamy, p. 11; Stephen Dalton / Science Source, p. 11; Helmut Corneli / Alamy, p. 13; B.A.E. Inc. / Alamy, p. 13; Paulo Oliveira / Alamy, pp. 14, 19, 35; iStock Photo, pp. 16, 28, 32; Nature Picture Library / Alamy, pp. 16, 18, 60; Adisha Pramod / Alamy, p. 17; Howard Chew / Alamy, p. 19; Design Pics / Alamy, p. 30; Cultura Creative / Alamy, p. 31; © National Oceanic and Atmospheric Administration / Science Source, p. 39; Jeff Rotman / Alamy, p. 42; blickwinkel / Alamy, pp. 44, 59, 67; Torsten Dietrich / Alamy, p. 46; Dante Fenolio / Science Source, p. 54; Stocktrek Images, Inc. / Alamy, p. 55; Ross/Tom Stack Assoc / Alamy, p. 57; Frank Teigler/Hippocampus Bildarchiv / Alamy, p. 66; Konrad Zelazowski / Alamy, p. 69; Author photo courtesy of Linda Saxton

ISBN: Print 978-1-64876-800-2
eBook 978-1-64876-198-0
R0

Printed in China

CONTENTS

WELCOME, JUNIOR SCIENTIST!

You are about to dive deep into the amazing world of fish! In this book, you will learn some of the incredible facts scientists have discovered about the world's most abundant **vertebrates**: fish! You'll meet lots of unusual fish **species**, some that live deep in the ocean and some that live right near your home. You will learn about experiments you can do as a junior scientist to see what it's like to be a fish. You'll also get a peek at fishing, keeping aquariums, and fish-based jobs you can have, like being a fish scientist.

FISH BITE

The word "fish" can mean one fish or a bunch of fish. Scientists, who need to be as accurate and precise as possible, also use the word "fishes." For them, "fish" means one fish and also a bunch of the same species of fishes. "Fishes" means a bunch of different species of fish.

School of jackfish, page 15

PART I

FANTASTIC FISH

You've probably seen fish while fishing, visiting an aquarium, or eating in a seafood restaurant. You may even have fish as pets. As cool as those fish are, they're just a small part of the world's fish. Scientists have named more than 34,000 unique species! They even think there may be thousands of fish species we still haven't seen yet. We've discovered fish as small as a staple and fish that are bigger than a bus. Fish that look like snakes and fish that look like horses. Even fish that walk on land and fish that glide through the air. As you read this book, you'll get a closer look at the amazing diversity of these creatures.

What Is a Fish?

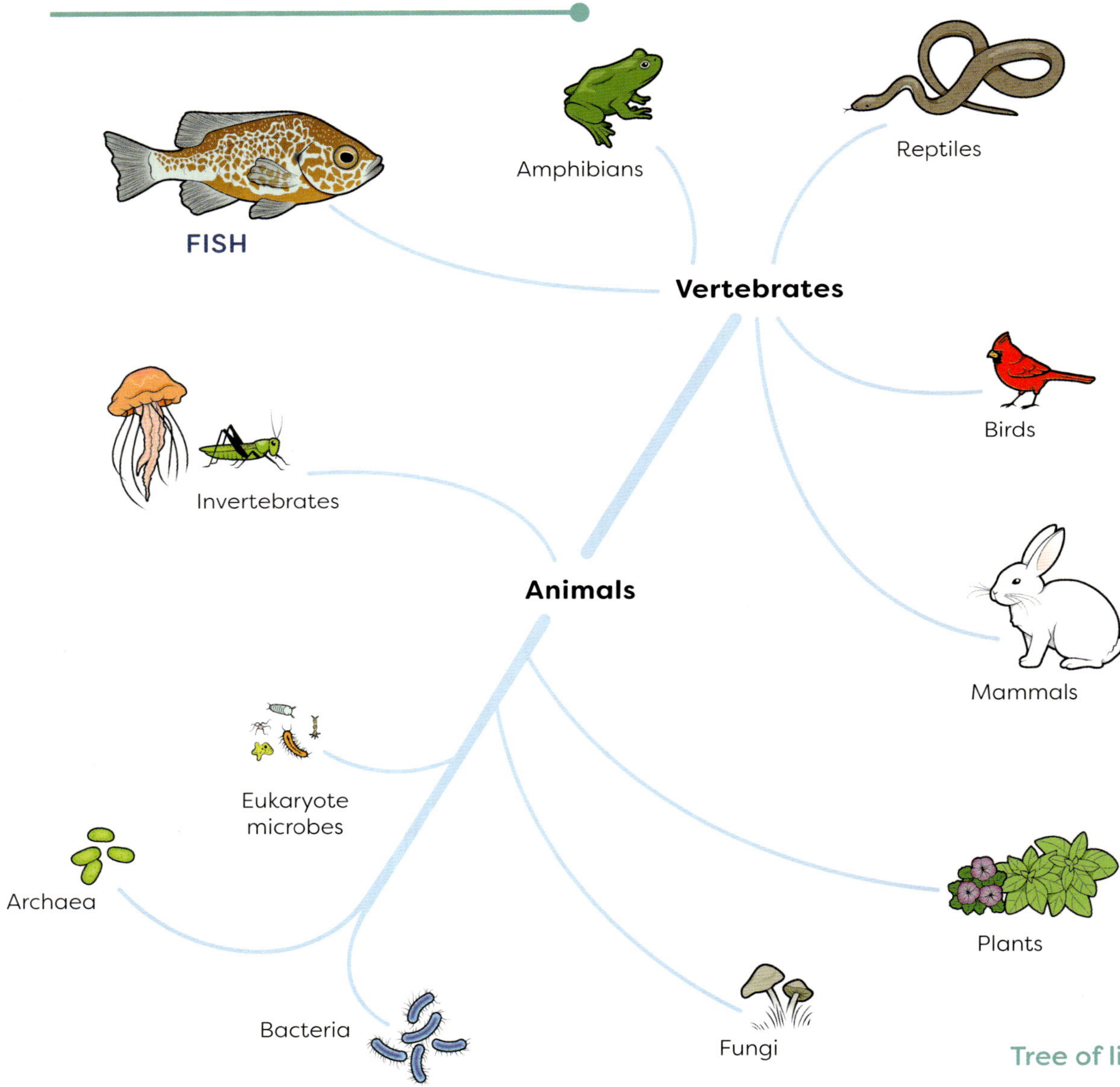

Tree of life

Fish are animals that:

- live underwater
- have a backbone
- have **gills** for breathing
- have no fingers or toes

An animal has to have all four of these to be a fish.

For example, dolphins are a vertebrate (an animal with a backbone) that lives in water. Dolphins do not have gills, though, so they are not fish. Horseshoe crabs have gills and live in water, but they are **invertebrates** (animals without a backbone), so they are not fish. Axolotl are salamanders that live in water, and they have gills and a backbone, but they have toes, so they are not fish.

Most fish also have other things in common. Fish typically have fins and scales. They also tend to be cold-blooded, meaning their bodies are the same temperature as the water around them.

FISH

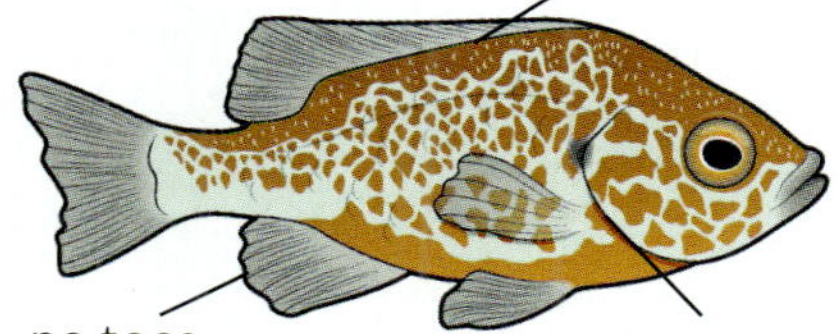

Pumpkinseed sunfish

NOT A FISH

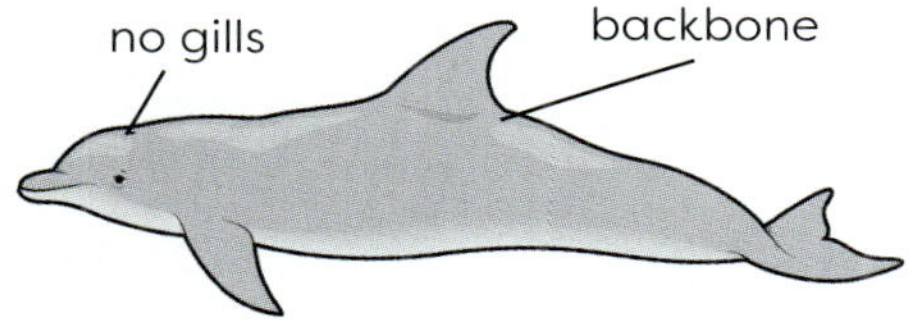

Dolphin

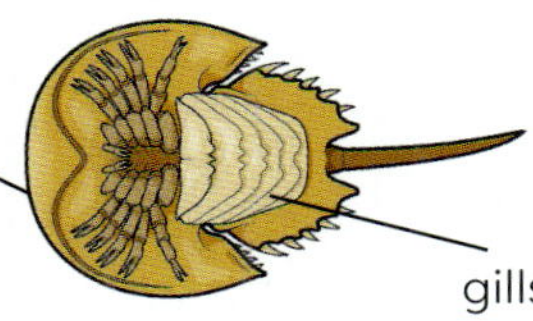

Horseshoe crab

Axolotl

> **FISH BITE**
> Bluefin tuna and salmon sharks are fish that are not cold-blooded. They can raise their body temperatures.

Ancient Fish

Cephalaspis lyelli jawless fish

Fish are the world's oldest vertebrates. They first appeared more than 500 million years ago. That is about 320 million years before mammals appeared!

The earliest fish could not bite anything because they did not have jaws. They sucked **algae** and other bits of food off the ocean floor.

Fish evolved jaws about 450 million years ago. Jaws allowed fish to catch and eat prey and to live in places away from the seafloor.

Though ancient fish share the same basic characteristics as modern fish, some could be pretty weird. There were armored fish (dunkleosteus), sharks with buzzsaw teeth (heliocoprion), and even the largest fish ever known to live (the 70-foot-long Leedsichthys). These fish species went **extinct** millions of years ago. We know about them today because they left behind **fossils**.

Types of Fish

Scientists have noticed that some fish species have more things in common with one another than they do with other species. Based on this research, they have determined there are three main types of fish.

JAWLESS FISH

Today, the only jawless fish left are hagfish and lampreys. Along with lacking jaws, these fish do not have scales or matching fins on either side of their body. Their skeletons are made of **cartilage**.

CARTILAGINOUS FISH

Cartilaginous fish have jaws and skeletons made of cartilage. The cartilaginous fish are sharks, rays, skates, and ratfish (yes, sharks are fish with skeletons made out of the same stuff as your earlobes).

JAWLESS

Brook lamprey

CARTILAGINOUS

Stingray

Great white shark

BONY

Blue surgeonfish

Barracuda

BONY FISH

Bony fish also have jaws, but their skeletons are made of bones. Bony fish are by far the most common type of fish. They include tuna, catfish, minnows, clownfish, bass, eels, anglerfish, seahorses, and many more. Along with skeletons made of bone, these fish have an operculum and a swim bladder. An operculum is a bony plate that protects the gills. Swim bladders are like little floats inside bony fish bodies. Swim bladders contain air that keep bony fish from sinking.

FISH BITE
The only cartilaginous fish fossils we usually find are teeth because their soft skeletons decay too quickly.

Fish skeleton

From Head to Tail

Fish come in a variety of sizes, ranging from Paedrocypris dwarf minnows, a fish that only gets to be less than a quarter of an inch (6 millimeters) long (smaller than a staple!) to whale sharks, which can grow up to 61 feet (19 meters) long! Fish come in a variety of shapes too. Some are round, flat, or even blob-like.

As diverse as fish are, they have a lot of body parts in common.

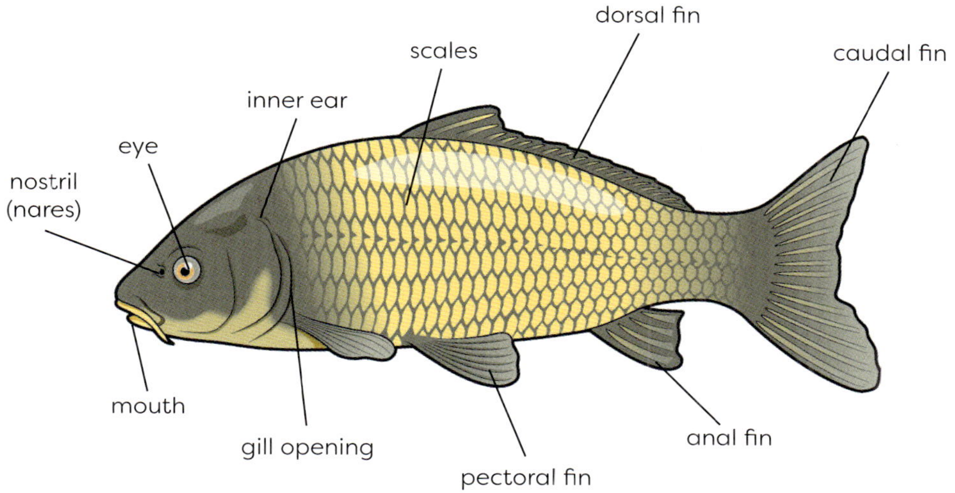

European carp

HEADS

A fish's head is connected to its body. They don't have a neck like yours. This gives fish a streamlined body shape. Like you, a fish's brain, mouth, and most of its sense organs are in its head. Fish have eyes for seeing, nostrils for smelling (though not for breathing because that's what gills do), and hidden inner ears for hearing.

FINS

Fish use fins to swim. Most fish have two **pectoral fins** on the left and right side of their body. They use these for steering. Their **caudal fins** on the tail push them forward through the water. The **dorsal fins** and **anal fins** on their belly and back keep them from wobbling.

SCALES

Many fish have scales all over their body. Scales overlap each other like shingles on a roof. They help protect a fish's skin.

FISH BITE
Fish don't really sleep. They don't have eyelids so they can't close their eyes. They will stop moving to give themselves time to rest, though.

Breathing in Water

Like all animals, fish need to breathe **oxygen** to stay alive. While you use lungs to breathe oxygen from the air, fish breathe oxygen underwater using gills. Gills work like a kitchen strainer. When you pour noodles into a strainer, the strainer collects the noodles but lets the water go through. A fish's gills collect the oxygen in the water but let the water flow through. The gills then put the oxygen in the fish's blood, so the oxygen can reach all the parts of the fish's body that need it.

Most fish open and close their gill openings to pump water into the mouth and over the gills. Some sharks, like great white sharks, can't do this, so they need to swim all the time to keep water flowing over their gills.

Gills of a fish

FISH BITE
Lungfish have lungs and gills. They use lungs to breathe air when the water around them dries up.

Swim Like a Fish

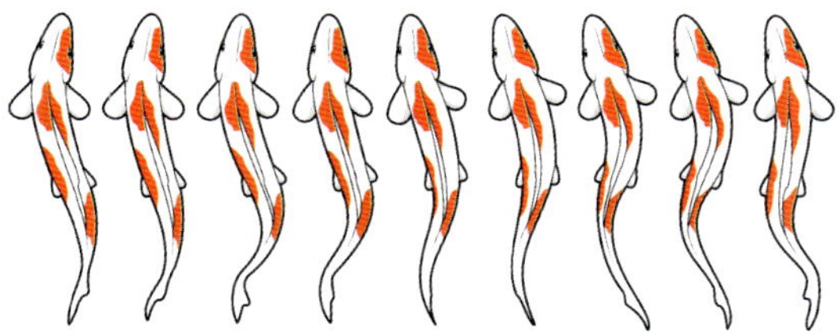

S-shaped swimming of fish

Most fish swim by waving their bodies side to side. If you were looking at these fish from above, their waving bodies make S-shaped curves. Fish with caudal fins on their tail also wave the caudal fin back and forth to push the fish forward.

The fastest fish, the sailfish, can use its caudal fin to reach speeds of almost 70 miles (112 kilometers) per hour!

Eels also wave their bodies in S-curves. They do not have caudal fins to push them forward, so they are slow swimmers.

The tail of a seahorse is built for gripping, so seahorses use their dorsal and pectoral fins on their sides and back to swim. They can wave these fins back and forth up to 70 times per second to move around.

Rays and skates also have a unique way of swimming. Their tails are too skinny to move them forward. Instead, they use their large pectoral fins. They flap these fins up and down and look like a bird while swimming.

FISH BITE
Parts of the pectoral fins of sea robins have evolved into "legs" they use for walking on the seafloor.

Fish Food

Fish eat lots of different things. Looking at the mouths and other body parts of a fish provides clues to what that species typically eats.

Fish with sharp teeth, streamlined bodies, and mouths facing forward, like sandtiger sharks and alligator gar, are good at chasing down and catching fish and other large swimming animals.

Other **predatory** fish that aren't as streamlined, like frogfish and flounder, are ambush hunters. They wait in hiding until prey gets close. Then, the fish surprises its prey and eats it.

Many fish, like anchovies and basking sharks, are **filter feeders**. They eat tiny floating plants and animals. Filter feeders open their large mouths to bring in water. They use filters in front of their gills to catch the tiny creatures in the water.

Alligator gar

Basking shark

Some fish species feed in unique ways. Seahorses wrap their tail around seaweed or coral to hold them in place. As the current carries plankton by, the seahorses suck them up with their long mouths.

Slender seahorse

Archerfish stick their mouths out of the water to spit at insects above them. The spit knocks an insect into the water so the archerfish can eat it.

Archerfish

FISH BITE

Sharks are much less dangerous than deer. Deer kill about 10 times as many people as sharks do. Each year, deer kill about 100 people and sharks kill about 10.

JUNIOR SCIENTISTS IN ACTION

Try this experiment to see how filter feeders catch food!

What you need:

2 CLEAR GLASS CONTAINERS (for example, 2 drinking glasses)

1 COFFEE FILTER

1 RUBBER BAND

1 TABLESPOON OF COFFEE GROUNDS OR DIRT

WATER

What to do:

1. Cover the top of one of the glass containers with a coffee filter. Wrap the rubber band around the coffee filter so it holds the filter tightly to the glass container.
2. Fill the other glass container halfway with water.
3. Pour the coffee grounds or dirt into the container of water.
4. Carefully pour the glass of water onto the filter so the water goes into the glass.

Think of the coffee filter as a filter in a fish's mouth, and the tablespoon of stuff in the water as plankton or tiny fish. How does a filter feeder catch its food? What do the filters do to the water?

Fish Protection

Fish have a lot of ways to protect themselves from **predators**. Here are just a few examples:

HIDE!

Garden eels dig holes in the sandy seafloor. They always keep part of their bodies in their hiding places so they can quickly duck into them if a predator shows up.

Garden eel

RUN AWAY!

To get away from predators, flying fish swim as fast as they can to build up speed and then burst out of the water. They then spread their pectoral fins like wings to glide through the air. Some flying fish glide more than 600 feet (183 meters) before they return to the water!

Flying fish

BE PAINFUL

Many fish have sharp bony spines in their fins that can jab into a predator's mouth. Some fish take this a painful step further. Scorpionfish can inject **venom** into a predator with their sharp spines. Surgeonfish have spines on their tail that are so sharp, they can slice into a predator like a scalpel.

Scorpionfish

BE A MOUTHFUL

When hagfish are bitten, they immediately secrete slimy mucus. The slime clogs up the predator's mouth and gills and causes the predator to spit out the hagfish.

Hagfish

FISH BITE

A truck carrying live hagfish crashed in 2017, causing the road and lots of cars to be covered in hagfish slime.

Schools of Fish

A group of fish traveling together is called a **school**. Fish that swim in schools can all turn at the same time. They have a sense organ called a **lateral line** that stretches from the gills to the tail. The lateral line is made of tiny hairs that feel movement in the water. It can feel the fish turning next to it. The fish then knows to turn in the same direction.

Schooling helps fish find food. With thousands of eyes looking around, it's a lot harder to miss something to eat.

All the eyes in a school are also looking for predators. If a predator attacks, it doesn't know which fish to chase. The predator's confusion gives all the fish in the school a better chance of escaping.

Lateral line

FISH BITE

Atlantic herring can form schools that have a quarter of a billion fish in it! If all those fish lined up, they could wrap around the Earth almost twice.

Fashionable Fish

Foureye butterflyfish

Fish come in a variety of colors and shapes. These differences help fish to survive in their **habitats**.

CAMOUFLAGE COLORS

Lots of fish use **camouflage** to blend in with their surroundings and stay safe.

Many fish are dark-colored on top and light-colored on their bellies. When predators beneath them look up, their white bellies blend in with the sunshine. When predators above them look down, their dark backs blend in with the darkness of the seafloor.

Shiny fish live near the surface of the water. Their shininess blends in with shimmering sunlight.

Some fish use both their color and their shape as camouflage. The body and color of sargassum fish look just like the seaweed *sargassum*. When

Sargassum fish

a sargassum fish is in sargassum, it is really hard to see it!

> **FISH BITE**
> The color red works like camouflage in the ocean. Most fish can't see red, so red fish look gray.

FLAT CHAMELEONS

Halibut and flounder are fish that are flat like a pancake. They can also change their color to match their surroundings. This allows them to hide on the seafloor and wait to ambush prey.

California halibut

BIG MOUTHS

It's hard to find prey in the **deep sea**, so many fish there, like anglerfish and pelican eels, use their huge mouths to get enough food to eat. Giant mouths allow deep sea fish to swallow prey almost as big as their bodies, because it might be a long time before they find more food.

Pelican eel

Life of Fish

Like all animals, fish have babies. But because there are so many different kinds of fish, the ways those babies are born and raised can be very different.

Fish typically go through four stages of life. First, most are eggs. They then hatch as **larvae** (they look like a tiny cross between a worm and the adult they will become). In the **juvenile** stage, they look like small adults. As adults, they are capable of having babies of their own.

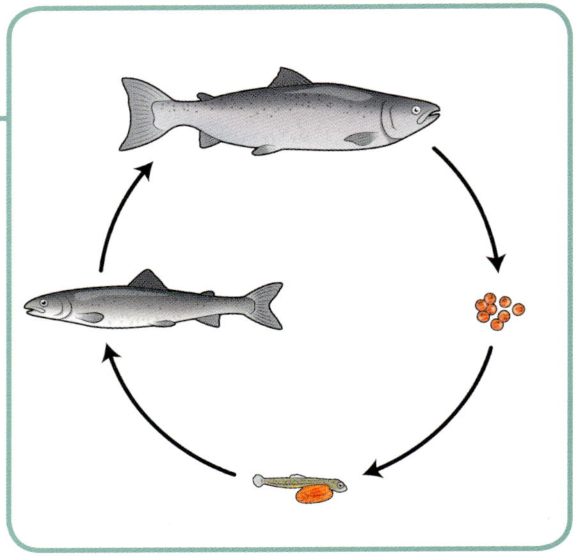

Fish life cycle

FISH EGGS

Fish eggs are not like bird eggs. They are usually soft, clear, and tiny.

Some cartilaginous fish, like spotted catsharks, lay eggs with tougher shells. The tough shell gives more protection than the average fish egg. The baby can grow inside the egg with a much better chance of not being eaten.

Spotted catshark egg

FISH AREN'T ALWAYS THE BEST PARENTS

For many fish, they are done with parenting after they lay their eggs. The tiny fish babies are on their own and lots of animals can eat them. Female fish may release millions of eggs at one time to increase the odds that at least some of them will survive.

Atlantic salmon eggs

FISH BITE

Some fish do not lay eggs. Guppies and many sharks give birth to live babies.

BUT SOME ARE GOOD CAREGIVERS

Some fish protect their eggs. A female seahorse lays its eggs in a pouch on the male's belly. He protects them until they hatch and enter the water. The males of yellowhead jawfish also protect their eggs, except they do so by keeping the eggs in their mouth!

Yellowhead jawfish

FISHEYE LENS: KEEPING AN AQUARIUM

You can keep fish inside your home with an aquarium, but it requires a lot of work.

An aquarium has to have the right kinds of air, food, water, shelter, and space for each fish that lives there. You will also need to make sure you choose fish that can live together. Each fish species has its own quirks about which other species it can live with, so you will need to do research.

Fish also need clean water. To keep the water clean, you will need to:

- install a filter
- change the water regularly to remove waste the filter misses
- make sure the tank doesn't have too many fish for the filter to handle
- not overfeed them, since the uneaten food creates waste
- regularly do water quality tests

Once you commit to doing all these things, then you need to decide if you want a freshwater or a saltwater tank. Saltwater fish can be more colorful, but they are much harder to keep (they are usually picky eaters). It's also a lot harder to keep the water quality healthy in a saltwater tank.

So, there is lot of research and work to do, but if you are willing to do that and your parents are willing to help, home aquariums can be a lot of fun.

Watery Homes

Fish live in a variety of underwater habitats. Most fish can only live in either freshwater or saltwater. Some fish can live in both.

FRESHWATER HABITATS

Freshwater habitats are surrounded by land. They get their water from rain and from groundwater (which is water that's found under the land's surface).

- Streams and rivers carry water quickly over land. Fish that live in streams and rivers, like trout, tend to have streamlined bodies. This makes it easier for the fast-moving water to flow past them.
- Ponds and lakes are places where freshwater collects on land and does not move quickly. Ponds and lakes tend to have shallow areas where plants and algae grow. Many fish use these weedy spots as hiding places.

Pond and lake zone

- Freshwater wetlands are places where freshwater floods onto land and partially covers the bottoms of trees, grasses, and other plants. Swamps, marshes, and bogs are all types of freshwater wetlands. Freshwater wetlands usually do not last long, so fish may only live in them for part of the year.

BRACKISH WATER HABITATS

Brackish water is saltier than freshwater, but not as salty as the ocean. The amount of salt in brackish water habitats changes with the tides.

- An **estuary** is a place where a freshwater river meets the ocean. Saltwater fish may come into estuaries only when it is high tide and

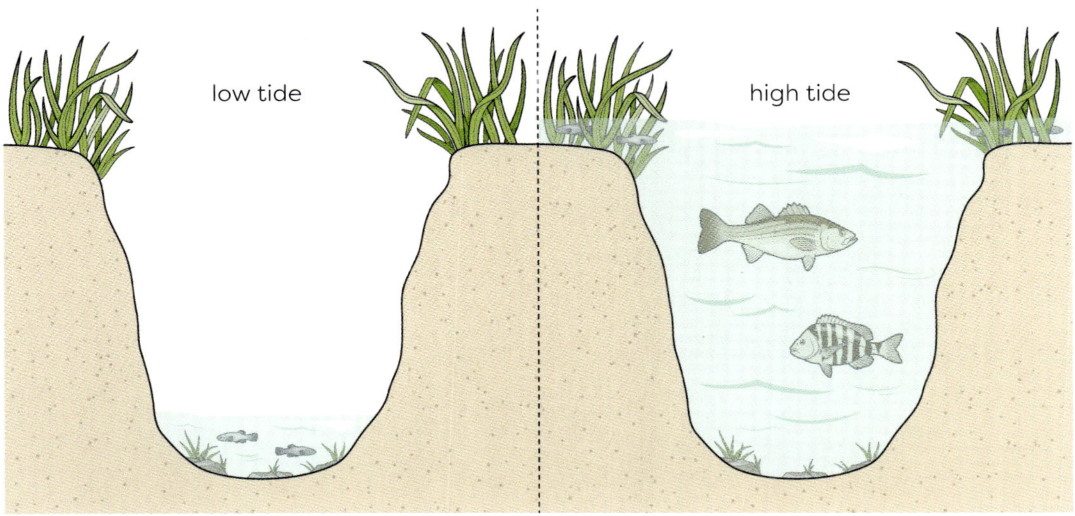

Salt marsh at low and high tide

the water is saltier. Some fish, like bull sharks, can live in both salt- and freshwater, so they can stay in estuaries all the time.

- Salt marshes and mangrove forests are places where water levels rise up and down with the tides of saltwater. Salt marshes have grass. Mangrove forests have trees. Big fish can only come in them during high tide. Little fish can hide there during low tide.

SALTWATER HABITATS

The ocean ranges from the shallow water you see at the beach to the depths of ocean trenches (the deepest part of the ocean is more than 35,000 feet or 10,668 meters deep!). So there are many different habitats in the ocean.

- Coral reefs are found in shallow, clear, warm waters. The reefs are made of the skeletons of invertebrate animals called corals. Colorful little fish feed off the live corals and the algae that grows on the reef. Big fish then eat those little fish.
- Kelp forests are places where a type of alga called kelp can grow 100 feet (30 meters) tall. Many small fish live in kelp forests to get food and shelter. This attracts larger predators, even great white sharks!
- Most of the ocean is open water. Fish in open water tend to be fast swimmers and swim in schools. They may also have camouflage colors that help them hide in water.

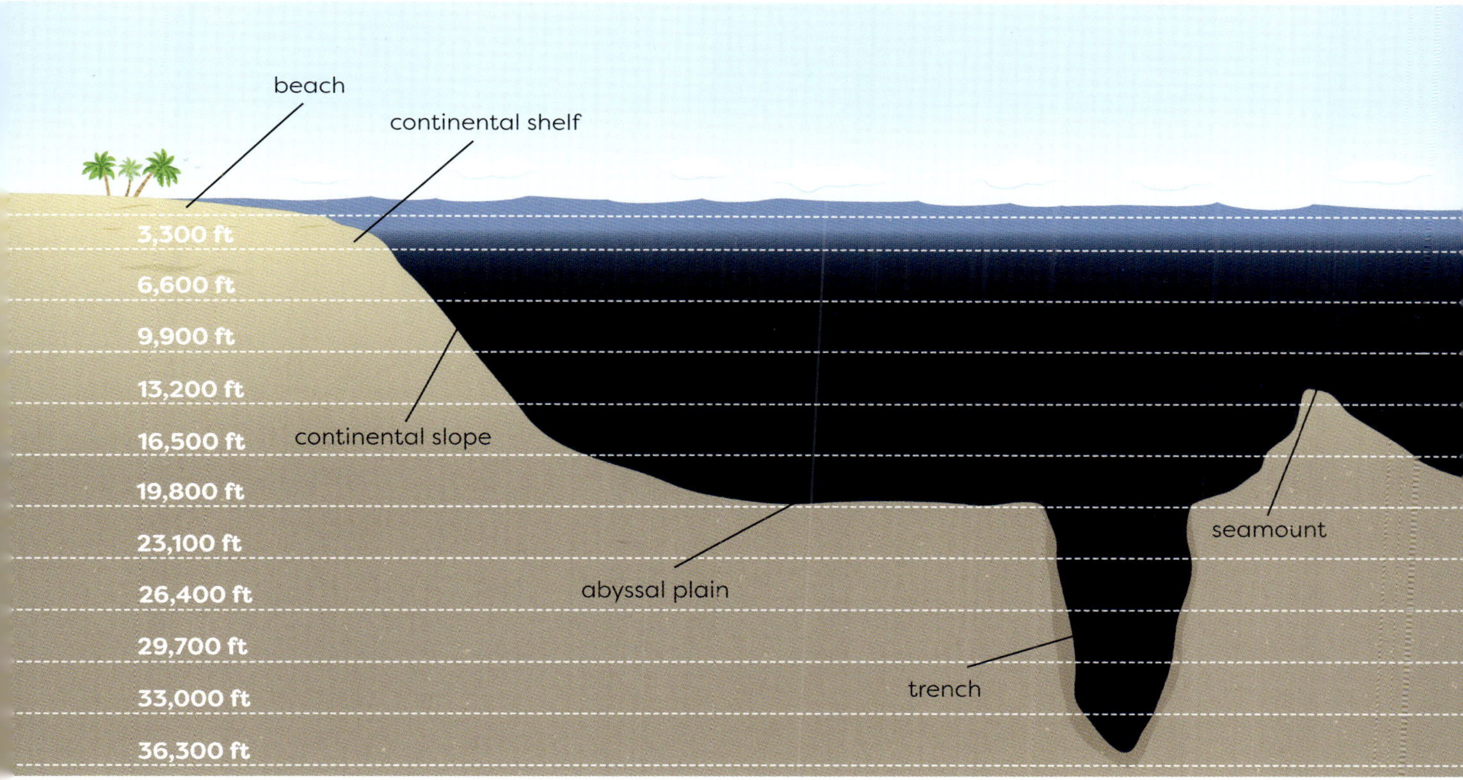

Layers of the ocean

JUNIOR SCIENTISTS IN ACTION

Try this experiment to see what happens when saltwater meets freshwater in an estuary!

What you need:

2 CLEAR PLASTIC CONTAINERS THAT CAN BALANCE ON EACH OTHER (for example, 2 drinking cups)

WATER

RED AND YELLOW FOOD COLORING (or whatever colors you have)

SALT

A THIN, STIFF PIECE OF PAPER, LIKE A CARD

What to do:

1. Fill both containers to the top with water.
2. Put a couple of drops of yellow food coloring in one container. Put a couple of drops of red food coloring in the other container.
3. Put salt in the yellow water (about ½ tablespoon per cup of water). Stir until the salt disappears.
4. Put the yellow saltwater container in a sink or bathtub.
5. Put the card on top of the red freshwater container.
6. Quickly, but carefully, flip the red freshwater container over onto the yellow saltwater container, while holding the index card on top of the red container to hold the water in.

7. Carefully pull out the index card.

What happens? How quickly do the fresh- and saltwater mix? Why do you think this happens? (Hint: It has something to do with **density**.)

Here's what happens: Though the saltwater and the freshwater have the same amount of water in them, the saltwater also has a lot of salt in it. Because it has more stuff in the same amount of space, it is *denser* than the freshwater. This causes the freshwater to float on top of the saltwater for a little while. Eventually they start mixing together to make brackish water.

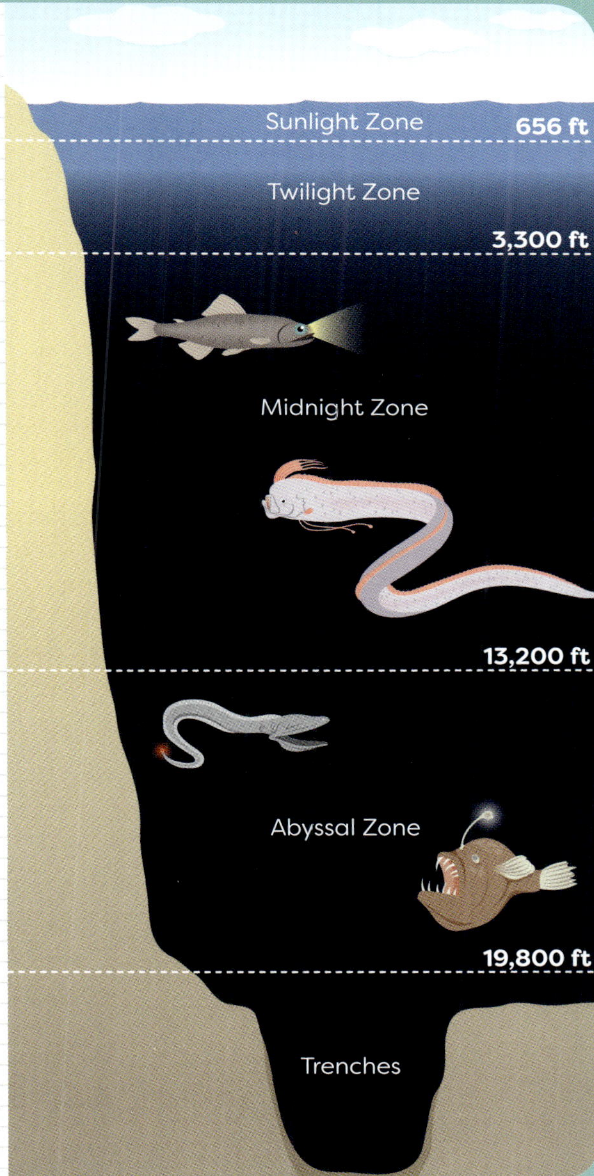

Helpful Fish

Fish, like all animals, have an important role in nature.

Many underwater animals eat fish. Land animals like grizzly bears, bald eagles, and humans eat fish, too.

Fish are also predators and **scavengers**. Predator fish keep other animal populations from getting out of control and hurting habitats. By eating dead stuff, scavenger fish clean up freshwater habitats and the ocean.

Some fish don't just help their habitat in general. They help individual fish get through their day. Small fish like wrasses and gobies are "cleaner fish." They eat parasites and dead skin off larger fish to "clean" them. Cleaner fish are so helpful that large fish will gather in "cleaning stations" and wait for their turn to be cleaned.

Cleaner fish

Fish Conservation

People can cause problems for fish. These can include:

- **Overfishing** (people catch fish faster than fish can have babies to replace themselves)
- Pollution (dangerous chemicals and plastic garbage wash into water habitats)

- Climate change (air pollution causes temperatures to rise, which warms up normally cool water habitats)
- Loss of habitat (people build on wetlands, dams are built on rivers that block fish migrations, too many snorkeling tourists damage coral reefs, etc., which all take away homes from fish)

People are also coming up with **conservation** solutions to these problems. Some of these solutions are:

- Having rules for how many fish can be caught each year
- Banning single-use plastics like straws and grocery bags
- Making rules that reduce air pollution
- Creating marine sanctuaries and natural reserves that protect habitats

Plastic garbage floating in the ocean

FISH BITE

There are many jobs you could have that work with fish. Some examples are fish scientist (ichthyologist), aquarium animal caretaker, aquarium educator, commercial fisherfolk, fisheries manager (a person who decides when fish are in danger of being overfished), and seafood chef.

FISHEYE LENS: HOW TO FISH

Fishing is a great way to see fish. Here are a few tips to get you started:

- Find out your local fishing rules, such as which fish you are allowed to catch and how many.
- Get a fishing license, if you need one.
- Go fishing around sunrise or sunset. This is when fish are most active.

- Fish hang out where the water temperature is just right. In spring and fall, you should fish in shallow water where the water is warmer. In the middle of the summer, fish will move to deeper, cooler water, so that's when you may need a boat.
- Your bait should look like something the fish wants to eat. Live worms work well,

but avoid the biggest worms. They're easier for fish to steal off your hook.

- Fish like to hang out in weeds, but if you cast your line there, your hook may get snagged. Instead, cast right next to the weeds. It won't get snagged, and it may catch the attention of the hiding fish.
- Be patient. Fish aren't going to be racing to bite your hook. But, if you're willing to wait, fishing can be a lot of fun.

Pufferfish

PART II

FISH UP CLOSE

Water covers 71 percent of our planet. Earth's water contains a variety of habitats for fish. In this section, we will look at 35 amazing fish species from different freshwater and saltwater habitats around the world. Some of these fish may live near your home. Some may live on the other side of the planet. We'll look at the incredible ways these different fish eat, protect themselves, have babies, and more!

Alewife

Scientific name: Alosa pseudoharengus

SAY IT! *ah-LOW-zah sue-doe-HA-rain-goose*

Alewife are one of about 200 species of herrings. They are fished for food, but also to be used as bait and as fertilizer on farms. The fish oil in tablets that people take for health reasons often come from alewife and other herring species.

Alewife live in the ocean as adults but swim into freshwater rivers and streams when they lay their eggs. In the last 100 years, alewife have been introduced into many landlocked freshwater lakes. There are now many alewife who spend their entire lives in freshwater. These landlocked alewife still travel into rivers and streams to lay their eggs.

FISHY FACTS

DISTRIBUTION/RANGE: Freshwater and saltwater habitats in eastern North America from Canada to South Carolina

HABITAT: Shallow ocean, estuaries, rivers, and lakes

SIZE: About 12 inches (30 centimeters) long

DIET: Animal plankton and small fish

LIFE SPAN: Up to nine years

American Eel

Scientific name: Anguilla rostrata

SAY IT! *an-GWEE-la row-STRAH-tuh*

American eel are the only freshwater eel in North America. They are a target of **commercial fishing** for food to the point that they are now overfished.

Adult eel live in freshwater habitats, like lakes and rivers, but they lay their eggs in the ocean. They may swim hundreds of miles to reach the Sargasso Sea, a place in the middle of the Atlantic Ocean between North and South America that is filled with sargassum seaweed (see page 16 to learn more about sargassum). The adults die after laying eggs. When the eggs hatch, the babies travel toward land to live in freshwater habitats.

American eel can breathe through their skin. This allows them to travel on land if they need to.

FISHY FACTS

DISTRIBUTION/RANGE: The Atlantic Ocean, Caribbean Sea, and Gulf of Mexico along the coast of North America

HABITAT: Freshwater, brackish, and ocean habitats

SIZE: Up to 60 inches (150 centimeters), but typically around 20 inches (50 centimeters)

DIET: Almost anything, including fish, algae, and dead animals

LIFE SPAN: 10 to 40 years

Atlantic Bluefin Tuna

Scientific name: Thunnus thynnus

SAY IT! *THUN-us THEEN-us*

Atlantic bluefin tuna are the largest of the 15 tuna species. They are popular for food and for commercial and **recreational fishing**. They are so popular they have unfortunately been overfished.

Bluefin tuna can reach speeds of 45 miles (72 kilometers) per hour. Despite their speed, predators like orcas and mako sharks will catch and eat them. Like many smaller fish, bluefin tuna form schools to help them escape predators.

Bluefin tuna are one of the only fish that can make the insides of their bodies warmer than the water around them. Because of this, they can live in both tropical water and in the chilly waters of the North Atlantic that are too cold for most tropical fish.

FISHY FACTS

DISTRIBUTION/RANGE: Across the Atlantic Ocean

HABITAT: Open ocean waters

SIZE: Up to 15 feet (4.6 meters) long and 1,500 pounds (680 kilograms)

DIET: Small schooling fish like anchovies, as well as squid and crabs

LIFE SPAN: Up to about 30 years, but typically about 15 years

Atlantic Sturgeon

Scientific name: Acipenser oxyrinchus

SAY IT! *ah-chee-PEN-sir ox-ee-RINK-coos*

Atlantic sturgeon are one of more than 25 species of sturgeon. Sturgeon eggs are eaten by humans (the name for the fish eggs we eat is "caviar").

Dams can be a problem for Atlantic sturgeon. Adult Atlantic sturgeon live in the ocean, but they swim into freshwater rivers to lay eggs. When dams are built on rivers, they block the fish from going upstream. This means the sturgeon can't lay their eggs. Sturgeon disappear in places that have too many dams.

Atlantic sturgeon are called "living fossils." Like prehistoric fish, they have bony plates (called "scutes") around their body for protection. Most modern fish do not have scutes.

FISHY FACTS

DISTRIBUTION/RANGE: Coastal habitats from Canada to Florida

HABITAT: Shallow ocean, estuaries, and freshwater rivers and lakes

SIZE: Up to 170 inches (430 centimeters), but typically about 100 inches (250 centimeters) long

DIET: Invertebrates like clams, shrimp, and insects

LIFE SPAN: Up to 60 years

Betta Fish

Scientific name: Betta splendens

SAY IT! *BAY-tah SPLEN-dens*

There are more than 70 species of betta fish.

Betta fish use bubbles to build nests. They gulp air and then cover the air with mucus. They stick the mucus bubbles together to make a nest. When the female lays her eggs, the male grabs the eggs with his mouth. He spits them all inside the bubble nest, which gives the babies a safe place to develop.

Betta fish will fight each other if one invades the other's territory. In the wild, these fights only last a couple minutes until the loser swims away. In an aquarium, there is nowhere to swim. Betta fish in a tank will fight until one or both die.

FISHY FACTS

DISTRIBUTION/RANGE: Freshwater habitats in Thailand, Cambodia, Laos, and Vietnam

HABITAT: Ponds, wetlands, rice fields, and along large rivers

SIZE: About 3 inches (7.5 centimeters) long

DIET: Insect larvae, animal plankton, insects that fall in the water, and algae

LIFE SPAN: Up to two years

Blobfish

Scientific name: Psychrolutes marcidus

SAY IT! *sigh-crow-LOO-tess mar-CHEE-dus*

Blobfish are deep sea fish that have become internet memes and were once voted the world's ugliest animal.

Those photos of cartoon-like blobfish are not what they actually look like when they are alive. In the deep sea, blobfish look like normal fish. Unlike fish at the surface, blobfish have soft bones, hardly any muscles, and bodies like jelly. This allows them to live in water pressure that can be more than 1,500 pounds (680 kilograms) per square inch (that's like having a cow stand on every square inch of a blobfish's body). When brought to the low pressure of the surface, they deflate and droop like a balloon that has lost most of its air, which is what makes them look so ugly-but-cute.

FISHY FACTS

DISTRIBUTION/RANGE: The deep sea around Australia

HABITAT: Ocean waters 2,000 to 3,900 feet (600 to 1,200m) deep

SIZE: Up to 12 inches (30 centimeters) long

DIET: Small shrimp, crabs, and other invertebrates

LIFE SPAN: Scientists aren't sure yet

Brook Trout

Scientific name: Salvelinus fontinalis

SAY IT! *sal-VEE-leen-us fon-tea-NAIL-iss*

Brook trout are actually a species of char. Char are closely related to trout and salmon. Brook trout are popular for **fly fishing**. A fishing "fly" is a fishing hook that is made to look like the insects a fish likes to eat.

Unfortunately, fish farms are causing problems for brook trout. The fish farms put other fish, such as brown trout and rainbow trout, into the brook trout's native habitats. They do this so fisherfolk have more trout to catch.

Brook trout need to be in cool waters to survive. They can survive all over the northeast United States. In the hot southeast, they can only live in the cool streams of the Appalachian Mountains.

FISHY FACTS

DISTRIBUTION/RANGE: Native to freshwater habitats in eastern Canada and the United States

HABITAT: Freshwater streams, rivers, and lakes

SIZE: Up to 34 inches (86 centimeters) long, but typically about 10 inches (26 centimeters) long

DIET: Insects, invertebrates, as well as small fish, amphibians, and mammals

LIFE SPAN: Up to 24 years

Channel Catfish

Scientific name: Ictalurus punctatus

SAY IT! *ICK-ta-la-roos punk-TAH-tus*

Channel catfish are one of more than 3,400 known species of catfish in the world. They are popular for fishing and as food for people.

Channel catfish dig a small hole in the sandy ground to make a nest. The female lays up to 50,000 eggs there. Both parents work together to guard the eggs.

Channel catfish have taste buds on their "whiskers" and all over their body to find food in dark and murky water. Because of all the taste buds on them, some people call channel catfish a "swimming tongue."

FISHY FACTS

DISTRIBUTION/RANGE: Fresh-water and brackish water habitats in North America

HABITAT: Lakes, ponds, rivers, and streams

SIZE: Up to 26 inches (67 centimeters) long

DIET: Crayfish, clams, snails, algae, frogs, and even small fish, birds, and mammals

LIFE SPAN: Up to 40 years, but typically about 14 years

Clearnose Skate

Scientific name: Raja eglanteria

SAY IT! *RAH-jah egg-lon-tay-REE-ah*

Clearnose skate are one of more than 150 species of skates. Skates look like and are closely related to rays. The differences are skates have thicker tails and smaller teeth than rays. Skates do not have stinging spines on their tail. Clearnose skate got their name because part of their snouts are see-through.

Clearnose skate hunt on the seafloor. Their mouth is on the bottom of their bodies, making it easier to bite animals below them. They have about 100 hard, flat teeth in their mouth that they use to crack open the shells of invertebrates.

FISHY FACTS

DISTRIBUTION/RANGE: Coastal areas of the western Atlantic Ocean and Gulf of Mexico

HABITAT: Shallow brackish water and saltwater habitats

SIZE: Up to 31 inches (80 centimeters) long

DIET: Shrimp, clams, and other invertebrates, as well as small fish

LIFE SPAN: Up to 14 years

Common Lionfish

Scientific name: Pterois volitans

SAY IT! *TEAR-oh-iss VOL-ih-tans*

Common lionfish are popular aquarium fish. Some people have released lionfish in the Atlantic Ocean and Caribbean Sea from their home aquariums. These former pets have become a major problem because they are taking over habitats from native fish.

All lionfish have venom in their spines to protect themselves from predators. If a person gets stung by a lionfish, it can hurt for days.

Lionfish sometimes hunt together. A lionfish flaps its fins to tell another lionfish it wants to go hunting. If they see something, both lionfish spread out their fins to corner the prey. Then, they both eat it.

FISHY FACTS

DISTRIBUTION/RANGE: The western Pacific Ocean and eastern Indian Ocean, from southern Japan to Australia

HABITAT: Saltwater, shallow reefs

SIZE: 6 to 18 inches (16 to 45 centimeters long)

DIET: Small fish, shrimp, and crabs

LIFE SPAN: Up to 10 years (in the wild)

Common Shiner

Scientific name: Luxilus cornutus

SAY IT! *LUKE-see-loose core-NEW-toos*

Common shiners are one of about 1,500 species of minnows. Fisherfolk catch common shiners to use as bait for fishing.

Male common shiners get bumps on their head called "tubercles." These bumps let the females know the male is ready to make a nest. The males make the nest on the riverbed by moving stones around with their nose. Common shiners will also sometimes lay their eggs in the nests of other fish. Once the eggs are laid, the male and female leave them.

Common shiners do not have teeth in their mouth. Instead, they chomp up their food with teeth in their throats.

FISHY FACTS

DISTRIBUTION/RANGE: Freshwater habitats east of the Rocky Mountains in Canada and the United States

HABITAT: Streams and small rivers

SIZE: Up to 7 inches (18 centimeters), but typically about 3 inches (8 centimeters) long

DIET: Algae and insects

LIFE SPAN: Up to six years

Dwarf Gourami

Scientific name: Trichogaster lalius

SAY IT! *TREE-show-gas-ter LA-lee-oos*

Dwarf gouramis are popular aquarium fish. Like other aquarium fish, the pet store versions have been bred to be much more colorful than wild dwarf gouramis.

Male dwarf gouramis make a floating nest out of bubbles and bits of plants. To get a female to lay eggs in the nest, a male dwarf gourami flares out his fins and does a swimming dance in front of the female. If she likes the dance, she lays about 600 eggs at the bottom of the nest.

In an aquarium, the male dwarf gourami needs to be removed from the tank after three days of guarding his babies. After that, he may decide he wants to eat them.

FISHY FACTS

DISTRIBUTION/RANGE: Freshwater habitats in Pakistan, India, and Bangladesh

HABITAT: Lakes and slow-moving streams

SIZE: Up to 3.5 inches (9 centimeters) long, but typically about 2 inches (5 centimeters) long

DIET: Algae and small invertebrates

LIFE SPAN: Up to six years (in captivity)

Firemouth Cichlids

Scientific name: Thorichthys meeki

SAY IT! *THOR-ick-thees MAY-eek-ee*

Firemouth cichlid are one of at least 1,650 species of cichlids.

When a female lays eggs, the male firemouth cichlid chases away anything that gets too close to the eggs. To look scarier, the male flares out its red gills. This makes the two dark spots on its sides look like big eyes. This can trick other fish into thinking a much bigger fish is chasing them and they swim away.

In the wild, firemouth cichlid get their food by scooping up mouthfuls of mud. They sift through the mud to find invertebrates and bits of plants to eat. The dirt in the mud goes out their gill openings before they swallow the food.

FISHY FACTS

DISTRIBUTION/RANGE: Freshwater habitats in Belize, Guatemala, and Mexico

HABITAT: Rivers and sometimes streams in caves

SIZE: Typically, about 2.5 inches (6 centimeters) long

DIET: Algae, plants, and small invertebrates

LIFE SPAN: Up to 10 years (in captivity)

Freshwater Angelfish

Scientific name: Pterophyllum scalare

SAY IT! *tear-oh-FEEL-lum ska-LAR-ray*

Angelfish are found in the Amazon Basin. They are popular for freshwater aquariums.

In the wild, angelfish usually have shiny metallic scales with black stripes. In aquarium stores, angelfish can come in a variety of colors. All these different colors are the result of people breeding them in captivity.

Angelfish are fighters. The members of a group of angelfish will fight with each other to determine who is the top angelfish of the group. They will wrestle each other with their mouths and bash each other with their tails. The winner becomes the head angelfish.

FISHY FACTS

DISTRIBUTION/RANGE: Freshwater habitats in South America

HABITAT: Swamps and other flooded wetlands

SIZE: Up to about 6 inches (17.5 centimeters) long

DIET: Small fish, shrimp, and worms

LIFE SPAN: Up to 10 years (in captivity)

Giant Oceanic Manta Ray

Scientific name: Mobula birostris

SAY IT! *MOE-boo-la bee-ROW-strees*

Giant oceanic manta rays are one of two species of manta rays. They are the biggest rays in the world. Their wingspan can be 29 feet (9 meters) across. Manta rays do not have stinging spines on their tail.

Like most of the biggest animals in the ocean, giant oceanic manta rays are filter feeders. The "horns" of a manta ray, which are actually fins, guide plankton into the ray's mouth.

Giant oceanic manta rays sometimes jump completely out of the water. Scientists are not sure why they do this. They think they might be doing it to impress a potential mate, or even just for fun.

FISHY FACTS

DISTRIBUTION/RANGE: Warm ocean waters

HABITAT: Coastal saltwater habitats

SIZE: Up to 360 inches (910 centimeters) long but typically around 177 inches (450 centimeters), can weigh up to 6,600 pounds (3,000 kilograms)

DIET: Plankton and small fish

LIFE SPAN: Up to 40 years

Goldfish

Scientific name: Carassius auratus

SAY IT! *car-RAS-see-oos ow-RAT-toos*

Goldfish are a type of carp that are popular for home aquariums. Some people think the koi fish that are kept in decorative ponds are bigger goldfish. They are actually a different species of carp.

Goldfish have been kept as pets for more than 1,000 years. Though they are greenish-gray in the wild, they have been bred in captivity to have bright colors.

In the wild, goldfish are migrators. They may travel as much as 60 miles (100 kilometers) up or down a stream or river to lay their eggs.

FISHY FACTS

DISTRIBUTION/RANGE: Freshwater habitats in China, Japan, Laos, and Myanmar

HABITAT: Ponds, lakes, and slow-moving rivers

SIZE: Up to 9 inches (22 centimeters) long, but typically about 4 inches (10 centimeters) long

DIET: Plants and small invertebrates

LIFE SPAN: Up to 40 years (in the wild), but usually about 10 years

Great Barracuda

Scientific name: Sphyraena barracuda

SAY IT! *spee-RAY-nuh bare-uh-COO-duh*

Great barracudas are one of more than 20 species of barracuda. Although not many people eat barracuda, they are popular for recreational fishing.

Great barracudas can swim up to 35 miles (55 kilometers) per hour to catch prey with their mouth full of sharp teeth. Barracudas sometimes bite people, too, but it is rare. When people are bitten, it is usually because the person has something shiny that looks like a shiny fish. Barracuda also bite people who are **spearfishing** and holding bleeding fish.

Not many people eat barracuda meat because it can be poisonous. Barracudas eat fish that eat poisonous plankton. The poison travels up the food chain until it ends up in the barracuda.

FISHY FACTS

DISTRIBUTION/RANGE: Warm ocean waters

HABITAT: Coastal and open ocean saltwater habitats

SIZE: Up to 79 inches (200 centimeters) long, but typically around 55 inches (140 centimeters), can weigh up to 110 pounds (50 kilograms)

DIET: Fish

LIFE SPAN: Up to 14 years

Great White Shark

Scientific name: Carcharodon carcharias

SAY IT! *car-CHAIR-oh-don car-CHAIR-ee-as*

Great white sharks are one of more than 500 known species of sharks. They are popular villains in movies and TV shows. They are fished by people who want their body parts to show off. They are becoming overfished.

Female great white sharks make eggs, but they do not lay them. The eggs stay inside of a female great white shark's body until the babies hatch. Before a great white shark baby leaves its mother's body, it may eat the other eggs.

FISHY FACTS

DISTRIBUTION/RANGE: Ocean waters, except in the polar regions

HABITAT: Mostly along coastlines

SIZE: Up to 21 feet (640 centimeters) long and can weigh up to 6,600 pounds (3,000 kilograms)

DIET: Smaller sharks, stingrays, squid, and marine mammals like seals and porpoises

LIFE SPAN: Up to 36 years

Greenthroat Parrotfish

Scientific name: Scarus prasiognathos

SAY IT! *SCARE-us prah-see-ug-NAH-thus*

Greenthroat parrotfish are one of about 80 known species of parrotfish, which includes bullethead, yellowfin, palenose, and other colorful species.

Parrotfish have that name because of their parrot-like beak. They use the hard beak to break off chunks of coral that has algae growing on it. They have hard teeth in their throat that grind up the coral. They swallow the coral and the algae. The bits of coral they poop out become grains of white sand.

Trumpetfish will sometimes hide behind parrotfish. Because parrotfish are vegetarians, most fish aren't afraid of them. Trumpetfish use parrotfish to sneak up on prey.

Most parrotfish are born female, though many of the females will eventually turn into males.

FISHY FACTS

DISTRIBUTION/RANGE: The tropical region of the Indian and western Pacific Oceans

HABITAT: Saltwater shallow reefs

SIZE: Up to 27 inches (70 centimeters) long

DIET: Algae

LIFE SPAN: Up to seven years (in the wild)

Guppy

Scientific name: Poecilia reticulata

SAY IT! *poe-ee-CHEE-lee-ah ray-tick-coo-LA-tah*

In the wild, there is only one species of guppy. Like dogs, they have been kept as pets for a long time and have been bred into many varieties. There are currently more than 300 varieties of guppies, but they are all the same species. The colors and shapes of the "fancy" guppy don't exist in the wild.

It is easy to tell a male guppy from a female guppy. Females are all gray, while males have colorful patterns they use to impress the females. Full-grown females can be twice as big as full-grown males.

Guppies don't lay eggs. They have live babies. The babies need to move away pretty quickly, because guppy parents sometimes eat their babies.

FISHY FACTS

DISTRIBUTION/RANGE: Northeast South America

HABITAT: Freshwater streams, rivers, and ponds

SIZE: Usually about 1 inch (3 centimeters) long

DIET: Mostly small insects

LIFE SPAN: About two years (in the wild)

Humpback Anglerfish

Scientific name: Melanocetus johnsonii

SAY IT! *may-la-no-CHAY-tus JON-sun-ee*

Humpback anglerfish are one of more than 200 known species of anglerfish. Anglerfish are famous for being really scary-looking, even though they are smaller than a volleyball.

Anglerfish use the light in their lure to attract prey. The rest of their body is hidden in the darkness. When the prey is close enough, the anglerfish grabs the prey and eats it.

Female anglerfish are much bigger than the males. Males only grow 1 inch (3 centimeters) long. A male humpback anglerfish bites hold of a female's stomach, so he is with her when she is ready to lay her eggs. He lets go once the eggs are laid. For most other anglerfish species, the male bites into a female's stomach and stays there for the rest of his life. He lives off the female like a parasite.

FISHY FACTS

DISTRIBUTION/RANGE: Oceans in warmer areas

HABITAT: Deep sea habitats up to 14,765 feet (4,500 meters) deep

SIZE: Up to 7 inches (18 centimeters) long

DIET: Fish

LIFE SPAN: Scientists aren't sure yet

Largemouth Bass

Scientific name: Micropterus salmoides

SAY IT! *me-CROP-tear-oos sail-MOY-dess*

Largemouth bass are one of nine species of black bass. There are many other fish species that are also called "bass," but they are not as closely related.

When largemouth bass first hatch from their eggs, the babies form a school. The father will guard the school until they have grown to 1 inch (3 centimeters) long. This takes about a month.

Largemouth bass are predators that eat almost any animal that fits in their mouth. They have eaten snails, salamanders, snakes, bats, birds, baby alligators, and other largemouth bass.

FISHY FACTS

DISTRIBUTION/RANGE: Native to freshwater habitats east of the Mississippi

HABITAT: Streams, rivers, swamps, ponds, and lakes

SIZE: Up to 38 inches (97 centimeters), but typically about 16 inches (40 centimeters) long

DIET: Fish, frogs, crayfish, and other small animals

LIFE SPAN: Up to 23 years

Leafy Seadragon

Scientific name: Phycodurus eques

SAY IT! *FEE-co-doo-russ AY-coos*

Leafy seadragons are popular aquarium fish, but they are disappearing in the wild. One reason is too many people have been taking them out of the wild to put them in aquariums.

Like their cousins the seahorses, seadragon males carry eggs in a pouch on their stomach. About 250 eggs stay there. They hatch in about nine weeks. Once the babies leave the male's pouch, they are on their own.

The color and shape of leafy seadragons make them look like seaweed. The leafy parts that stick out of their body are not fins. They are just for camouflage to help them hide.

FISHY FACTS

DISTRIBUTION/RANGE: The Indian Ocean along the southern coast of Australia

HABITAT: Shallow saltwater seaweed near reefs

SIZE: Up to 14 inches (35 centimeters) long

DIET: Animal plankton

LIFE SPAN: Up to seven years

Map Pufferfish

Scientific name: Arothron mappa

SAY IT! *AIR-oh-thron MAH-pa*

Map pufferfish are one of more than 120 species of pufferfish.

To protect themselves, puffers can quickly fill their stomachs with water or air. This expands their body like a balloon until it is too big for the predator's mouth. Some puffer species have spikes that stick out when their body puffs up.

Puffers are also extremely poisonous. The poison makes them taste really bad and is so toxic it can kill many fish—and humans, too. Chefs who prepare pufferfish have to train for years on how to remove the poison before they can serve pufferfish safely.

Pufferfish have strong teeth they use to crack open the shells of invertebrates like crabs and clams.

FISHY FACTS

DISTRIBUTION/RANGE: The tropical regions of the Indian Ocean and western Pacific Ocean

HABITAT: Saltwater shallow reefs

SIZE: Up to 26 inches (65 centimeters) long

DIET: Algae and small invertebrates

LIFE SPAN: Up to 10 years

Neon Tetra

Scientific name: Paracheirodon innesi

SAY IT! *pair-ah-KAY-row-don in-NAY-see*

There are dozens of fish species given the name "tetra" but they are not all closely related.

Neon tetras are the most popular fish for home aquariums. On average, almost 2 million of them are brought into the United States each month to sell in pet stores. Some of those were raised in fish farms in Asia. Others were caught in the wild in South America.

The colorful stripes of neon tetras may help protect them in the wild. In clear water, the stripes reflect off the surface above the tetra. A predator may chase the reflection while the real tetra escapes.

FISHY FACTS

DISTRIBUTION/RANGE: Northwestern Amazon Basin in South America

HABITAT: Freshwater streams

SIZE: Usually about 1.5 inches (4 centimeters) long

DIET: Plants and small invertebrates

LIFE SPAN: About two years (in the wild)

Northern Pike

Scientific name: Esox lucius

SAY IT! *AY-socks LOU-choos*

Northern pike are one of seven species of pike in the world. They are popular for recreational fishing.

Northern pike are ambush hunters. They float in the water without moving at all. Smaller fish swim close to a pike without seeing it is there. Then they get attacked. Some northern pike live in arctic lakes with no other fish species. In those habitats, the bigger pike feed on the smaller pikes.

Northern pike often get parasites like tapeworms. When fisherfolk catch a pike, it needs to be cooked for a long time. If the cooking doesn't kill the tapeworms, the people eating the pike can get tapeworms, too.

FISHY FACTS

DISTRIBUTION/RANGE: Freshwater habitats in northern North America, Europe, and Asia

HABITAT: Lakes and rivers

SIZE: Up to 60 inches (150 centimeters), but usually about 16 inches (40 centimeters) long

DIET: Mainly fish, but also frogs and crayfish

LIFE SPAN: About 24 years

Ocean Sunfish

Scientific name: Mola mola

SAY IT! *MO-la MO-la*

Ocean sunfish are the world's heaviest bony fish. They may also be the weirdest looking. To get that big, they have to eat a lot of jellyfish. A 265-pound (120 kilogram) ocean sunfish eats about 154 pounds (70 kilograms) of jellyfish a day.

Ocean sunfish will swim to coral reefs and kelp forests to get cleaner fish to eat the parasites off them. Some ocean sunfish even lie on the surface of the water to get seagulls to eat their parasites.

A female ocean sunfish can lay up to 300 million eggs each year. When released, each egg is barely big enough to see. Out of the 300 million eggs an ocean sunfish releases each year, only two of them may make it to adulthood.

FISHY FACTS

DISTRIBUTION/RANGE: Oceans around the world, except the polar regions

HABITAT: The open ocean

SIZE/WEIGHT: Up to 11 feet (3.3 meters) long and can weigh up to 2.5 US tons (2.3 metric tons)

DIET: Mainly jellyfish

LIFE SPAN: Scientists aren't sure yet

Orange Clownfish

Scientific name: Amphiprion percula

SAY IT! *am-fi-PRY-on PUR-cue-la*

The orange clownfish is just one of more than 30 known species of clownfish. They are popular aquarium fish.

Clownfish have a special relationship with sea anemones in which they live together and help each other. Clownfish live in the anemone's stinging tentacles. The sting keeps predators away. Clownfish have a special slime on their bodies that blocks the sting from hurting them. Clownfish help sea anemones by being messy eaters. The food they drop feeds the sea anemone.

Orange clownfish tend to live in groups of about five fish. The biggest fish is always female and the rest are males. If the female dies, the biggest male will turn into a female!

FISHY FACTS

DISTRIBUTION/RANGE: The western Pacific Ocean near Australia and New Guinea

HABITAT: Saltwater, shallow reefs

SIZE: 2 to 4 inches (5 to 11 centimeters) long

DIET: Tiny shrimps and crabs

LIFE SPAN: Up to 10 years (in the wild)

Red Discus

Scientific name: Symphysodon discus

SAY IT! *sim-FEE-sew-don dis-coos*

Red discus are one of three species of discus fish. Discus fish in pet stores are much more colorful than the same species in the wild. They are bred in captivity to look flashy.

Discus fish put more effort into raising babies than the average fish. Both parents guard the nest of eggs and then protect the babies for a couple of weeks after they hatch. They even feed the babies. This might sound gross, but the babies eat the slime that comes out of their parents' skin.

Discus fish live within groups of 10 to 12 discus fish. Because of this, they won't survive long in a home aquarium if they don't have any discus fish friends.

FISHY FACTS

DISTRIBUTION/RANGE: Freshwater habitats in the Amazon

HABITAT: Swamps, lakes, and rivers

SIZE: Up to 5 inches (12 centimeters) long

DIET: Algae, plants, and small invertebrates

LIFE SPAN: Up to 15 years (in captivity)

Sockeye Salmon

Scientific name: Oncorhynchus nerka

SAY IT! *own-core-INK-oos NARE-kuh*

Sockeye salmon are one of eight species of salmon, seven of which live in the Pacific Ocean.

All sockeye salmon return to the freshwater stream, river, or lake where they were born to lay eggs, even if they have to jump over waterfalls to get there. Some streams can be clogged with hundreds of salmon swimming upstream. Sockeye salmon die after laying eggs.

Sockeye salmon are the only species of salmon that are filter feeders. The pink color of their meat comes from the pink krill that it eats.

FISHY FACTS

DISTRIBUTION/RANGE: Coastal waters around the northern Pacific Ocean

HABITAT: Open ocean waters and freshwater lakes, streams, and rivers

SIZE: Up to 33 inches (84 centimeters)

DIET: Small shrimp and insects

LIFE SPAN: Up to eight years, but typically four to five years

Southern Stingray

Scientific name: Dasyatis americana

SAY IT! *DAH-see-ah-tiss uh-mare-ih-CON-uh*

Southern stingrays are one of more than 225 species of stingrays.

Southern stingrays are bottom feeders, which means they eat animals that live in the sand and mud on the seafloor. Like sharks, stingrays sense electrical impulses from other animals. Stingrays use this to find buried prey. Cormorants, a type of bird, will follow hunting stingrays and eat the fish the stingrays kick up from the sand.

Hammerhead sharks and other predators eat stingrays. To hide from them, stingrays will bury themselves with just their eyes above the sand. If they are found, they will lash out at the predator with the sharp, venomous spike on their tail.

FISHY FACTS

DISTRIBUTION/RANGE: Coastal areas of the Western Atlantic Ocean

HABITAT: Shallow saltwater and brackish water habitats

SIZE: Up to 79 inches (200 centimeters) long but typically around 35 inches (90 centimeters), can weigh up to 300 pounds (136 kilograms)

DIET: Small fish, crabs, and other invertebrates

LIFE SPAN: About 12 years

Tiger Barb

Scientific name: Puntigrus tetrazona

SAY IT! *PUN-tee-groos tet-rah-ZONE-ah*

Tiger barbs are a species of barb fish. Barbs are closely related to goldfish and other carps. There are 70 species of barbs that are sold for home aquariums.

In the wild, tiger barbs are schooling fish. Tiger barbs in a home aquarium will need other tiger barbs in their tank so they can form a school. If the aquarium only has one or two tiger barbs, they become aggressive and will bite other fish—and your fingers if they can.

The name "barb" comes from the Latin word for "beard." Most species of barb fish have bumps under their chin called "barbels." Barbels are sense organs that feel what is underneath the fish. Barbels can make a fish look like it has a beard.

FISHY FACTS

DISTRIBUTION/RANGE: Freshwater habitats in parts of western Indonesia and Borneo

HABITAT: Streams

SIZE: About 2.5 inches (7 centimeters) long

DIET: Plants and small invertebrates

LIFE SPAN: About 6 years

Variable Platyfish

Scientific name: Xiphophorus variatus

SAY IT! *see-FOE-four-us var-ee-AH-toos*

Variable platies are one of 26 species of platyfish. They are popular fish for home aquariums.

Platyfish may be causing problems in the wild. People who no longer want platys in their home aquariums have been releasing them into local streams in many countries. The platys quickly populate the new habitats, because they have babies faster than most fish. All those platys might then take food, shelter, and space away from native fish species.

Platies have mouths that point upward. This makes it easier to bite and eat things that are above them.

FISHY FACTS

DISTRIBUTION/RANGE: Freshwater habitats in Mexico

HABITAT: Streams and warm springs

SIZE: About 1.5 inches (4 centimeters) long

DIET: Plants and small invertebrates

LIFE SPAN: About 3 years in captivity

White Cloud Mountain Minnow

Scientific name: Tanichthys albonubes

SAY IT! *TAN-ick-thees AL-bow-noobs*

White cloud mountain minnow are a type of carp. They are popular for home aquariums but are very rare in the wild.

When streams became too polluted, they started to disappear. No one was able to find any of them for 20 years. Many people thought they had gone extinct in the wild. Recently, small populations have been found in a couple of streams.

They were first discovered in the 1930s in China by a Boy Scout leader named Tan Kam Fei. In honor of his discovery, part of their scientific name, *Tanichthys*, means "Tan's fish."

FISHY FACTS

DISTRIBUTION/RANGE: Freshwater habitats in China and Vietnam

HABITAT: Mountain streams

SIZE: About 0.75 inches (2 centimeters) long

DIET: Small invertebrates and bits of plants

LIFE SPAN: About five years

Zebrafish

Scientific name: Danio rerio

SAY IT! *DAN-ee-oh RARE-ee-oh*

Zebrafish are one of more than 25 species of a type of fish called danios.

All zebrafish are born as females. When they are about five weeks old, some of them start turning into males.

Because zebrafish don't take up much space and they are quick to grow up and have babies, they are often used for scientific research, including medical research. Even though they look a lot different from us, zebrafish share 70 percent of the same genes as humans (genes are like our body's computer code that tell our bodies what to do). They have helped scientists learn more about diseases that affect humans, like muscular dystrophy and even cancer. Zebrafish could help people go to Mars! Scientists are studying what happens when zebrafish hibernate to see if astronauts could do the same thing during their long spaceflight.

FISHY FACTS

DISTRIBUTION/RANGE: Freshwater habitats in Pakistan, India, Bangladesh, Nepal, and Myanmar

HABITAT: Streams, ponds, and rice fields

SIZE: Up to 1.5 inches (4 centimeters) long

DIET: Small invertebrates

LIFE SPAN: Up to five years (in captivity)

Garden eel, page 13

MORE TO EXPLORE

APPS

TOCA NATURE APP

Available for iOS and Android

This world-building app allows kids to create underwater habitats and see how changes affect the fish and other animals that live there.

BOOKS

KURTZ, KEVIN. ***A DAY IN THE DEEP***. MOUNT PLEASANT, SC: ARBORDALE PUBLISHING, 2013.

In this book, kids explore deep sea habitats and the weird fish that live there, like cookiecutter sharks, viperfish, and pelican eels.

MAAS, DAVE. ***KIDS GONE FISHIN': THE YOUNG ANGLER'S GUIDE TO CATCHING MORE AND BIGGER FISH***. BEVERLY, MA: COOL SPRINGS PRESS, 2001.

This book helps kids learn fishing tips and techniques.

PARKER, STEVE. ***DK EYEWITNESS BOOKS: FISH***. LONDON, UK: DK CHILDREN, 2005.

A book about all kinds of fish.

DOCUMENTARIES

BLUE PLANET AND ***BLUE PLANET II***

These BBC Earth documentaries show amazing fish from around the world in their natural habitats.

WEBSITES

MONTEREY BAY AQUARIUM: ANIMALS A TO Z WEBSITE

MontereyBayAquarium.org/animals/animals-a-to-z

Learn about the fish and other ocean animals that are featured at the Monterey Bay Aquarium.

MONTEREY BAY AQUARIUM RESEARCH INSTITUTE (MBARI) YOUTUBE CHANNEL

YouTube.com/channel/UCFXww6CrLAHhyZQCDnJ2g2A

See amazing videos taken by scientists of deep sea fish and other animals.

NATIONAL GEOGRAPHIC KIDS: FISH WEBSITE

Kids.NationalGeographic.com/animals/fish

This website is a great introduction to fish.

SMITHSONIAN: OCEAN WEBSITE

Ocean.SI.edu

Learn about ocean fish and the different ocean habitats where they live.

GLOSSARY

ALGAE: A living thing that is simpler than a plant, but like plants, algae make food using sunlight; most seaweeds are algae

ANAL FINS: Fins that stick out from the bottom of a fish, which help keep them from swaying back and forth when they swim

BRACKISH WATER: Water that is saltier than freshwater but less salty than ocean water

CAMOUFLAGE: When the color and shape of an animal help it blend in with its surroundings

CARTILAGE: A rubbery tissue found in human earlobes and shark skeletons that is both firm and flexible

CAUDAL FINS: The tail fins of a fish, which it moves side to side to push it forward through the water

COMMERCIAL FISHING: Fishing done to catch huge amounts of fish in order to make money

CONSERVATION: The prevention of the loss of wildlife and habitats to make sure they last into the future

DEEP SEA: The part of the ocean that starts about 3,250 feet (990 meters) below the surface and can be as much as 35,000 feet (10,668 meters) deep

DENSITY: A measurement of the amount of stuff that fills a given space; things that are less dense will float on top of things that are more dense

DORSAL FINS: Fins that stick out from the top of a fish, which help keep them from swaying back and forth when they swim

ESTUARY: A place where a river meets the ocean and freshwater and saltwater mix

EXTINCT: When a species completely dies out so there are no members of the species left

FILTER FEEDERS: Animals that get their food by bringing lots of water into their mouth and then filtering out the tiny plants and animals in the water to eat

FLY FISHING: A type of fishing where the hook is decorated to look like something the fish wants to eat (called a "fly")

FOSSILS: The remains of a living thing that lived long ago

GILLS: An organ on the sides of a fish's head that takes oxygen out of the water so the fish can breathe

HABITAT: An environment that provides a living thing with the air, food, water, and other things it needs to survive

INVERTEBRATE: An animal without a backbone, such as jellyfish, crabs, squid, and insects

JUVENILE: A stage in life when a young animal is starting to look like an adult, but they can't yet have babies

LARVAE: A stage in life when an animal hatches from an egg but is still developing; larvae tend to look like tiny worms

LATERAL LINE: A sense organ on fish that stretches from the gills to the tail and feels movement in the water

OVERFISHING: When people take fish out of their habitats through fishing much faster than the fish can have babies to replace themselves; this causes species to start disappearing

OXYGEN: A type of gas that most living things need to survive; animals use oxygen to turn the food they eat into energy their body can use

PECTORAL FINS: The two fins on the sides of fish that they use for steering

PREDATOR/PREDATORY: An animal that catches and eats other animals

RECREATIONAL FISHING: Fishing done for fun, relaxation, or to provide food for a small group of people

SCAVENGERS: Animals that eat dead animals

SCHOOL: A group of the same species of fish that swim together for protection

SPEARFISHING: A type of fishing where divers swim underwater and use spearguns to spear and catch fish

SPECIES: A group of living things that look similar to each other, can have babies together, and their babies will be able to have babies

VENOM: A toxic substance that an animal injects into another animal to hurt or kill it

VERTEBRATES: Animals with a backbone, such as fish, amphibians, reptiles, birds, and mammals

INDEX

T

V

W

Y

Z

ABOUT THE AUTHOR

KEVIN KURTZ is an award-winning children's author who specializes in books about science and nature. He has worked at both a marine biology lab and an aquarium and got to spend a lot of time hanging out with fish. Kevin lives in Rochester, New York, where he continues to write books and offer school programs to introduce kids to the wonders all around us. Learn more about him at KevKurtz.com.